THE

STRENGTH

IN

OUR

SCARS

BIANCA SPARACINO

THOUGHT
CATALOG
Books

Published by Thought Catalog Books, a publishing house owned by The
Thought & Expression Company. Cover design by Josh Covarrubias
and art direction by KJ Parish and Chris Lavergne. It was printed in
2018 and published in an edition of 3,000 copies.

ISBN 978-0-9964871-9-1

I am a firm believer in there being beauty in the contrast. In the light and the dark days. In the hope and the hurt. In the fire and in the ash. I am a firm believer in the fall and in the rise; in the sin and in the saving. I am a firm believer in the broken, the people who hold their pieces together with belief, who bandage their fear in faith. I am a firm believer in the souls who have always managed to protect their soft; who have always known, even when it ached the most, that their wounds were healing them, that the hardest parts of life were growing them from the inside. I am a firm believer in there being beauty in the contrast—you have not lived until you have died.

The world is going to give you beauty,
but it will also give you pain.

The greatest lesson you will ever learn
is that this, too,
is a gift.

It is all I have lost
that has set me free.

It is difficult to move on. It breaks you down in ways you never expected to be broken before. But when this happens, do not fear the rebuilding. Do not lament the pieces of yourself that you have lost, the pieces of yourself that were left over. Instead, splay them across the kitchen floor. Look at each and every one of them. Look at the memories, look at the sacrifices. Look at it all from a place of healing, and choose to create yourself again. Shape your spine, stronger this time. Shape your heart, bigger this time. Shape your eyes, capable of seeing more than you ever imagined. Shape your mouth; give it the capacity to say all of the words you never allowed yourself to say. Begin again.

Your body is more than just a graveyard for those who could not love it. Your heart is more than just a cemetery for those who disappeared.

I am not impressed by beauty anymore. It is not difficult or extraordinary to turn someone on. However, if you have the ability to inspire me, if you have the ability to stimulate my mind and stir my thoughts—well, *that makes you magic.*

You are the one
who built your walls.

Don't ever doubt for a second
that you have the capacity
to tear them down.

Goodbye is hard sometimes because the action of leaving is so permanent, and yet that person still occupies so much of the space within your chest. Goodbye isn't final, it isn't a finish line you have to step over in order to forget. See, you can't unlove someone. You can't get their scent out of your pillowcases, can't unlearn their name and forget what it felt like to be immersed in the hope and beauty of another human being. People never stay gone. They show up in street corners, they show up in familiar laughs and the booth at that one restaurant where you first held their hand. Goodbye isn't as simple as many make it seem; goodbye isn't really goodbye, not for someone who still cares. Not for the person left in the aftermath of a hurricane they once loved.

You do not always have to be fire,
do not always have to burn
those who come too close.

Remember—
you are seventy percent water;
you have it within you to be soft.

From time to time, trace the scars life has left you. It will remind you that at one point, you fought for something. You believed.

The moment you truly start to believe that you are deserving of happiness, of love, of something bigger than what you have been settling for, your heart weeps a little—as if it is the first time in years it has been able to lay down its arms; as if it is the first time in years it has been able to rest.

Life has taught me
that the people who often love the hardest
are the ones who have been hurt the most.

It took me a long time to realize that not everything in life is meant to be a beautiful story. Not every person we feel something deep and moving with is meant to make a home within us, is meant to be a forever. Sometimes, people come into our lives to teach us how to love; and sometimes, people come into our lives to teach us how *not* to love. How *not* to settle, how *not* to shrink ourselves ever again. Yes, sometimes people leave—but that's okay, because their lessons always stay, and that is what matters. That is what remains.

Please, whatever you do—just feel what you are feeling right now. Do not reach into yourself and pull out what life has planted within you. Instead, reach into yourself and cradle it. Give it a home within you. Let is stay for as long as it needs. Do not rush it out the door. Just be with it. Whatever it is—whether it is a name, or a memory, or an ache that you cannot seem to part with. Do not harden yourself to what has affected you so deeply in life. This is the important part. Be thankful for it. Be thankful for the songs you hear that make your soul bubble over with nostalgia. Be thankful for the morning light and how it hits that one spot on your bed that holds the ghosted memory of someone who was once your favorite thing. Be thankful for your heart and how at one point, you could feel it beating against your rib cage for ten days straight because your bones were blushing at the thought of someone's hand within yours. Let these moments seek refuge in your soul. Let them wash over you. Let them remind you that at one point, you embraced what it meant to love without abandon. Let them remind you that at one point, you tried for something.

I will know my work is done
when they ask:
"Do you like yourself"
and with ruthless confidence,
with a certainty that comes
from every tender part of who I am,
I answer,
"yes."

They didn't leave you because they didn't love you. They left because when they were fourteen they had their best friend come to them with a heart that never healed. At fourteen they held a human being, trembling and broken in their paper arms, and they feared the day they would mourn a last goodbye, a last embrace. They left because they saw how a cold flame could create a house fire in the hollow bones of someone who gave every inch of themselves and still came up short.

No, they didn't leave you because they didn't love you. They left because when they were seventeen they finally noticed the distance between their parents at the dinner table. At seventeen they had to tell their younger brother, sister, that sometimes things get tough, that sometimes mistakes hang heavy in a rib cage and it causes people to run away. They left because at a tender age they were taught that "I love you" doesn't always mean, I'll stay."

They didn't leave you because they didn't love you. They left because at twenty-one they read an article about a dating app that mentioned how 42% of its users already had partners. At twenty-one they read that plan Bs and second options were always on the forefront, always in the back pocket of someone who was holding the hand of a man, a woman, who slept soundly beside them at night. They left because they convinced themselves that there would always be another, someone better suited, someone better looking, someone more successful; it would only ever be a matter of time.

See, they didn't leave you because they didn't love you. They left because at twenty-five they watched their grandfather empty out the oceans within him at the grave of his high-school sweetheart. At twenty-five they watched how he slowly deteriorated, how loss crept into his heart like a bleak December frost; how the doctor said that her demise killed him before old age ever had the chance. They left because they finally understood how cruel it truly was to love something that death could touch.

Trust me when I say they didn't leave you because they didn't love you. They left you because they never learned that they could be better than their past. They left you because they couldn't convince themselves that they wouldn't turn into their parents, that they wouldn't wake up one day and want to flee. They left you because they never saw devotion win, they never saw passion triumph.

No, they didn't leave you because they didn't love you. They left you because they didn't love themselves enough to believe that they could be different.

How they make you feel
says a lot about them
and nothing about you.

Trust me when I say
someone who makes you question
if you are worthy of being loved
is not worthy of being loved by you.

In a world that seeks connection, we oddly avoid eye contact, we time our text responses in order to protect ourselves from seeming too eager or too interested, and we hold our feelings back because we don't want to seem overly emotional or unreasonable. We silence our instincts, and at the end of the day instead of feeling good about ourselves, we feel alone, we feel misunderstood. Remember—it is okay to be emotional, to seek help, to confidently tell someone you enjoy being around that you are infatuated with them. There is nothing wrong with vulnerability, with being human, for that is what creates depth within our relationships, and that is what ultimately unifies us.

We use fate as an excuse,
as an apology for all of the people
we have walked away from;
we speak the years from our minds,
and say, "if it was meant to happen, it would have."
But we are wrong,
because fate does not exist;
only effort does.
and that is where we fail each other.
Because if it was meant to happen,
we would have made it happen.
If it was meant to be,
we would have stayed.
We would have fought.

If you are ever going to survive, if you are ever going to come out of the chaos, you have to collect the moments that have inspired you deeply in life and fold them into yourself every night for safekeeping. When the sun seems to rise a little slower and your days are filled with darkened hope, reach into the core of you and remember the warmth. Remind yourself that things will be light again.

You can say you have healed
not when you have forgotten,
but when you have forgiven.

There is still time for you. I don't care what you have been through; I don't care about the wounds or the pain or the scars or the hurt. None of that makes what you are a waste, none of that discounts the fact that you have purpose, that you mean something. Please, don't ever forget—even when you ache all over, even when the world is not kind—you are needed here. You are needed.

You guard yourself from sadness,
not realizing
that you have closed yourself off
to all of the happiness
the world is trying
to give to you.

Stay open;
it is how the light gets in.

Because you have been hurt before, you fall in love with anyone who shows you their soul. You know how much courage that takes.

Do not be ashamed of what your survival looks like. Do what you have to do. You are clawing yourself out of the ache, cutting the pain from the bone. It is never going to be pretty, but I promise—it will always be worth it.

The things that hurt you
may have left scars,
but they did not destroy you.

You survived,
and there is hope in that.

If you care about someone, make them a priority. Make them a priority not just when it is easy, but when it is difficult as well. If you care about someone, show up for them when you say you will. Show up for them when they least deserve it, because that is when they need it the most. Just be there for them—not because you have to be, but because you want to be. See, the easy things in life hold no weight. It is easy to love someone when they are perfect, when they are soft and light, when they are filled with hope and happiness. But loving someone when they are wearing their flaws like an apology, when they are breaking down, or when they are carrying hurt within them—that is when it means the most. That is when you must show up for them.

If you care about someone, put your phone down. Sit across from them at dinner and listen to them. Give yourself the space to dive with them into deeper conversation, into the kind of quality time that makes you feel like you are the only two people in the world. Connect with them. Please, if you care for someone—connect. Do not allow yourself to be pulled from those moments. Do not allow yourself to settle for talking about the weather or the monotony of life. Ask them what they dreamed about the night before. Debate with them. Teach them something new. Sit them down and laugh with them, lose yourself in time. Be present, not only in your body, but also in your mind. Be there with them.

If you care about someone, let them know that you do. Always remind them that you appreciate the very heart within their chest. Always remind them that you want to protect who they are, that they are your favorite thing, and do not just do this with words. See, words are simple; they are easy, they are flat. When it comes to someone else's soul, do not fill their head with silken poetry, do not string vowels and consonants together just to appease them. Show them that they matter to you; take action in making sure that they feel loved, in backing up what you speak.

If you care about someone, if you truly care, just be good to them. Too many people selfishly take hearts into their own hands and they fail to protect them, they fail to nurture them. Too many people grow comfortable and complacent; they lose sight of what they have. They take and take, and they rarely think about what they are giving. They forget that love is not something that should ever be done with one foot out the door. They forget that love should never be given in bare minimums.

Please, if you love someone, stand up for that. Be honest with them. Choose them every single day, and if you cannot, or if things change, let them go. Let them go, because if they love you deeply they will not have it within them to stop trying, they will not be able to walk away, for it is a fatal flaw in people who love with everything they have. They must be set free. Do not keep someone around only to love them in halves. They are better off giving their love to someone who has room within their chest to accept it, and you are better off figuring out what your heart desires before you try to open it to someone who will never stop trying to give you the world.

You are the only person who gets to decide if you are happy or not—do not put your happiness into the hands of other people. Do not make it contingent on their acceptance of you or their feelings for you. At the end of the day, it doesn't matter if someone dislikes you or if someone doesn't want to be with you. All that matters is that you are happy with the person you are becoming. All that matters is that you like yourself, that you are proud of what you are putting out into the world. You are in charge of your joy, of your worth. You get to be your own validation. Please don't ever forget that.

Stay soft.
Do not let the things that have hurt you
turn you into a person you are not.

All of the love you have given to
the wrong people—
it will find its way back to you.

"It's funny how that works," she said.

"The human body is made up of billions of cells, and yet it simply takes one person—one voice, one look, one text or smile, to completely unravel you. We think we are these overly intelligent, complex creatures, but at the end of the day we all just want connection. We all just want to know that we aren't going to be alone."

Listen—you are going to find the things that make you feel free in life. You are going to fall into the deepest love—with another human being and with yourself. You are going to discover the things that fill you with purpose, the things that make you want to rise each morning. You are going to feel hope cracking within all of the dark the past has buried within you; you are going to uncover all of that light. You are going to be okay. You are going to figure things out. But you must understand that there is no set timeline for this kind of discovery, there is no checklist for this kind of growth. You may fall in love tomorrow, or you may fall in love ten years from now. You might discover your passion the day after you graduate, or you might be fifty years old before you finally find the thing that causes your heart to ache with happiness. Whatever it is—just give it time. Be gentle with yourself; do not rush the way you stretch into the person you are becoming. Do not scramble to fill your life with things that are not for you just because you feel like you are falling behind. You are not falling behind—you are falling into your-self. So please, keep going. Everything that is meant to be yours will be yours. It will come. It will come.

The people who break you
are not the ones
who are going to put you back together.

I am not going to wait
for someone to make me whole.

Instead,
I am going to take all of the love
I have been giving everyone else,
and I am going to give
it to myself.

Lose yourself in books, in art, in the haze of new horizons. Lose yourself in curiosity, in knowledge, in passion. Lose yourself in feeling it all; lose yourself in the world, in the stories and the lessons it has to teach you, but never lose yourself in love; never lose yourself in another person. You are your own home—please don't ever forget that.

Be gentle with yourself;
you are still learning.

When you need to heal,
unhinge your ribcage.
peer into the soul of you,
find out where it hurts,
and quietly whisper into the ache—

"it's okay.
it's okay."

Listen—I know what it is like to have a heart that does not know how to stop burning, to have hands that want to give until they have nothing left. I know what it feels like to have firewood for fingers, what it feels like to want to touch every cold soul you see, what it feels like to want to reignite every bone in a body. I know what it feels like to be misunderstood within this—to be loved and unloved because of your heat; but you cannot give up on yourself, you cannot ignore all that surges within you. If the world does not understand the way you burn, do not hide yourself away.

Instead, set it on fire.
Show them what you can do
with all of that hope inside of you.

You are allowed to take up space. Own who you are and what you want for yourself. Stop downplaying the things you care about, the hopes you have. Own your passions, your thoughts, your perceptions. Own your fire. Stop putting your worth in the hands of others; stop letting them decide your value. Own saying no, saying yes. Own your mood, your feelings. Own your plans, your path, your success. Never back down from expressing yourself, from saying your name proudly. Never stop elbowing your damn way into this big world, because you belong here. *You matter.*

And I know that everything is temporary,
that all we have is fleeting—
emotions,
thoughts,
even human beings.
But it is hard not to get attached
to that which makes us feel like we have a purpose;
it is hard not to want to hold on
to all that makes us
feel real again.

One day you will meet someone who will break down your walls and stare into the depths of you. One day they will see the bruises on your soul, will hear about all of the terrible things you have done, and you will expect them to leave, but they won't. They won't. One day, you will meet someone who looks into the damage, who sees the wounds, the dark, and they will love you anyways. They will love you.

CONGRATS ON WAKING UP TODAY, FOR COURAGE IS IN THE LITTLE THINGS

Listen—sometimes courage is as simple as opening your eyes in the morning. Sometimes it's as easy as making the effort to eat your breakfast without spelling their name in your cereal or breaking your teeth on their goodbyes. Sometimes courage is the way you fall in love with your sadness, how you let it rock you to sleep, how you feel it and face it and tell yourself every single night that you can overcome it, even if you feel like you can't.

No, sometimes courage isn't a big declaration, a common accomplishment. Sometimes courage is the way you slowly comb them out of your hair; sometimes courage is hearing their voice in public and not turning your head or having your stomach feel like a shaken-up can of soda. Sometimes courage is smiling for your younger sister when your heart is breaking; sometimes it's telling her that love exists even on the days you simply don't believe it does.

See, sometimes courage isn't climbing Mount Everest or changing the world. Sometimes your mountain to climb is made up of weekdays and months, made up of pushing yourself forward even when you want to nestle into the past. Sometimes changing the world means changing your world as gradually as you need to, as gently as you heal, because sometimes courage isn't made up of war and bloodshed; sometimes courage isn't made of combat. Sometimes courage is a quiet fight, a dim softness within you, that flickers even on your darkest days and reminds you that you are strong, that you are growing—that there is hope.

Fall in love with someone who will take care of you—not in a materialistic way, but rather, fall in love with someone who will take care of your soul. Fall in love with someone who will take care of your mind, someone who will take care of your heart. Fall in love with someone who will take care of even the most chaotic parts of who you are.

Sometimes, healing consists of sitting in coffee shops and writing the years from your mind. Sometimes, healing is laughing until you cry; it is kissing your friends' faces and being moved and inspired by your life. And sometimes, healing is rest; it is hiding from the world, it is having everything inside of you be still and quiet and eerily bare. Sometimes healing feels like nothing at all, like you are a silhouette of hope and hurt at the same time. Do not fight it. Whatever your healing looks like today, whatever it consists of—just allow it to be what it is. Just take care of yourself.

Are there any rules
when it comes to love?
There is just one:

Let it change you.
Let it leave you better
than you were before.

Never lose sight of the fact that love,
and only love,
has the capacity to save
even the most desperate
parts of you.

Love is your childhood home. Your favourite part on the couch, the same chair at the kitchen table. Love is your worn-in sweater, the way it smells after you hang it to dry in the garden. Love is the creak in the stairs, the hook in the entryway you always hang your coat on. But leaving makes a mess of it all; it rearranges things. Suddenly, the couch is different, and your favourite chair is broken. Your worn-in sweater is torn, and the clothing lines in the backyard have been blown down by wind. Suddenly, the stairs are quiet in the night, the hook is on the other side of the room. Healing forces you to move. Forces you to buy a different couch, forces you to replace the chair. Healing stitches together your worn-in sweater, patches it with new fabric, pieces of another story. Healing forces you to embrace the silence in the steps, the fact that you have to hang your coat in a different place from now on. Healing forces you to change, to leave behind the familiar. Healing forces you to rebuild.

The truth is, when you continue to chase someone who does not want to be caught, you close yourself off to those who do. You close yourself off to the person who wants to know how many sugars you take in your morning coffee; you close yourself off to the soul that wants nothing more than to hear you singing off-key in the shower for the rest of their lives. When you continue to beg for the kind of love you have been giving someone all along, you close yourself off to the person who dreams of being your favorite thing; you close yourself off to the person who eagerly awaits a heart like yours—no matter how loudly it beats against your chest, no matter how messy or sensitive or soft it is. You close yourself off to the person who wants to be your safe place, your refuge; someone who wants to prove to you that love can stay, that love can heal the past, that love can be balanced and full and hopeful for once in your life. When you continue to chase those who do not want to be caught, you rip out pieces of your soul just trying to make it fit into the palms of someone who does not want to hold you. You bankrupt yourself for someone, closing yourself off from the human being who would have been able to see your worth all along; closing yourself off from the human being who would have loved you from the start.

Be brave enough to heal yourself
even when it hurts.

If you want to fall back in love with yourself—focus.

Focus on the things that compel you, the things that stir something deep inside of yourself.

Focus on the people who inspire you, the ones who support you and encourage you to grow into the person you have always wanted to be.

Focus on the things that hurt, the things that create noise in your life, and commit to distancing yourself from them. You have to be comfortable with walking away from the human beings and the thoughts that no longer serve you. You have to be comfortable with walking away from the chaos of it all.

Focus on the things that make you feel safe. The music, or the films, or the hands that make you feel like everything is blooming and awakening within you. Focus on the things that make you feel real, the things that make you feel whole.

Truly focus—on the things that make you feel hope, on the small spaces in time that make you feel like it is all going to be okay, like you have a reason and a purpose and a right to be in the world.

Just focus on the things that make you feel glad you are alive; focus on the things that feed your soul, and not only will you experience love—*you will become it.*

I hope you have the courage to walk away from any-thing that no longer serves you, from anything that fails to inspire your mind. I hope you have the courage to grow, to change, to do things differently than what is expected of you, to step back and seek out the kinds of things that ignite passion and excitement within your very bones. But most of all, I hope you have the courage to forgive yourself for all of the times you did not have the courage to believe that you deserved more than the kind of life you were settling for.

Some mornings you will wake up and your scars will ache, and some mornings you will wake up and you will fumble with all of the hope dripping from your fingertips. This is your growing, your healing, the balancing of the scales within your bones. You will be high and you will be low, but you will never be empty. You will never be empty.

HOW TO DEAL WITH SOMEONE LEAVING—HOW TO MOVE ON

Well—you will wake up to them everywhere, and yet they will not be there anymore. They are gone and you are here, alone with yourself again. But this is what you do. You brush them out of your hair. You wash them off of your skin. You cough their name out of your lungs, sweep the ash of their goodbye outside of the home that is your body. Let the wind blow them away. Close the door softly and cry. Wildly, like you are a storm, and remember—though the rain and the sadness may seem like terrible things right now, they are always cleaning you. They are always cleaning you.

I hope you find what you're looking for out there.

I hope you find the kind of happiness that exists on your own terms. I hope you truly take the time to figure out what moves you, what encourages your soul, what you deeply crave from life, and I hope you have the courage to chase that. I hope you have the courage to believe that you are deserving of everything you desire, that you are capable and worthy of curating the kind of life for yourself that sparks something within you. You have a fire inside of you—I hope you never let convenience, or comfort, or the easiness of standing still put it out. I hope you show the world what you can do with all of that passion inside of you.

I hope you find the kind of love that makes you a softer person. The kind of love that makes you want to be a better man or woman, the kind of love that believes in you and supports you, that stands by your side. I hope you find someone who quickly becomes your favourite thing—someone who makes the fall less fearful, someone you can't help but choose every single day. I hope you find someone who shows you just how deeply you can feel, just how deeply you can love. I hope you find something real, because nothing is more beautiful than loving someone who loves you back. Nothing is more beautiful than loving someone who builds you a home in their heart.

I hope you find acceptance. The kind that rings through your bones, the kind that quiets the voice inside of you that tells you that you are not good enough or that you are falling behind. I hope you forgive yourself for the mistakes you have made, for the past you keep alive inside of you. I hope you learn to let go—of the things you had to do in order to heal or to grow or to survive. You are doing your best. You are human. Please don't ever forget that.

I hope you find the kind of moments that take your breath away. The kind of moments that change you. I hope you travel to places that cleanse you; I hope you go to concerts that ring through your bones and make you feel alive. I hope you connect with the small things—I hope you look at someone mid-conversation and you feel your stomach surge with the feelings you have for them. I hope you surround yourself with the kinds of friends that encourage your spontaneity, that are always there for you. I hope you live. Truly. I hope you don't hold back. There is so much to feel in this world. I hope you feel it all.

But most of all, I hope you find yourself out there. I hope you figure out your heart, I hope you figure out your mind. I hope you learn how to be kind to yourself, how to embrace the journey you are on. I hope you learn how to be proud of the person you are becoming; I hope you learn how to be proud of where you are—even if it isn't exactly where you want to be. I hope you learn to fall in love with the process, with the messiness of life and the confusion of it all.

At the end of the day, I hope you find what you're looking for out there.

I hope your life inspires you.

If you are learning about yourself, if you are experiencing new things and flourishing inside, so is your heart; and your heart is allowed to recognize that at a certain point in time, it may deserve something different than what it once wanted. Remember—you are allowed to change. You are allowed to walk away.

You have dug your soul
out of the dark,
you have fought to be here;
do not go back
to what buried you.

Yes, your healing is your own. It is *your* battlefield, *your* war, but you do not have to fight it alone. See, it is not you against the world—it never has been. The people in your life may not be able to disappear the hurt, may not be able to cut the darkness from your bone—but they can stand by your side while you save yourself. They can love you through the pain of it all if you let them.

Let them.

If it matters to you,
if it is important to you,
then it is valid.

Think about all of the beauty
you would not have seen
if you had allowed yourself
to stop fighting;
if you had allowed yourself
to give up.

The truth is, you're not always going to be a good person. You're going to make a lot of mistakes. They will pile up within you and it will be in your nature to grip at them until your hands are bruised, but you must let them go. Please, let them go. One day you're going to see just how they conspired to grow you from the ground up. One day you're going to see how they never defined you; they only ever helped you to define yourself.

Sooner or later you are going to fall back in love with your life. Sooner or later your chest isn't going to weigh heavy like an anchor within your body. Sooner or later, you will remember the lightness, the days that didn't end in aching, and that is when you will realize it, that is when you will understand—*you survived*.

You don't need to look for the kind of love that patches your wounds and builds you a new home within your body. You can do that on your own. You have fallen and you have risen time and time again; you are the living, breathing fragments of your triumphs and your tragedies, stitched together through hurt and hope, and you still shine. You still shine.

Even at your best, you will not be good enough for someone who does not have the capacity, or the will, to love you. However, and this is the part you must focus on—none of that matters. For even at your worst, when you are not a shining example of everything you want to be, when life is handing you hardships and hurt, the person who is right for you will still choose you. Even when you do not deserve it, the person who is right for you will still love you.

Trust me when I say—when it is right, everything that you love ruthlessly will love you back with the same conviction. Trust me when I say—when it is right, the things you reach for in life, the things you deeply hope for, they will reach back. And I promise you, when that happens you will understand that all of the things you ached for that did not work out, all of the hearts that failed to appreciate the home you made for them inside of yourself, they were not the things that broke you, or ruined you, or made you less worthy. No, instead, you will see that they built you. They taught you about yourself. They led you to the person you were born to be, and they guided you to the person you were meant to be with. They shaped you. They challenged you. They grew you.

Be the person who cares. Be the person who makes the effort, the person who loves without hesitation. Be the person who bares it all, the person who never shies away from the depth of their feeling or the intensity of their hope. Be the person who believes—in the softness of the world, in the goodness of other people, in the beauty of being open and untethered and trusting. Be the person who takes the chance, who refuses to hide. Be the person who makes people feel seen, the person who shows up. Trust me when I say—be the person who cares. Because the world doesn't need any more carelessness, any more disregard; because there is nothing stronger than someone who continues to stay soft in a world that hasn't always been kind to them.

You're going to get hurt. There is no denying that.

You're going to thrust yourself into situations that don't work out the way you dreamed, that cannot sustain the gravity of what you feel, and you're going to get hurt.

But this is what your fear won't tell you—

You're going to survive it. You're going to heal from the wound. The hurt doesn't last forever, though I promise you the "what ifs" will. If you don't take the chance, if you don't risk everything you have—you will always be an ocean of questions. You will always wonder.

And trust me—life is too short for loose ends, for feelings that were never acted upon, gestures that were never taken. Get on the plane, send that person an I'm sorry, tell them you love them, drive all night to see someone in the morning. I don't care if it makes you vulnerable, if it exposes you. Expose yourself. Open the hell up. Let life fill you with hurt, with happiness; let it weather you, let it teach you. Let it inspire you, let it break you down and build you up. You are here to risk your heart. Please don't ever forget that.

Your heart is a fragile thing
that people have not handled with care,
but this does not mean
that you should turn around
and break someone
because you have been broken.

Do not become the kind of person
who hurts.

Do not let the world
make you hard.

If they walk away,
do not focus on the pieces of you that are missing,
do not focus on the empty;
the only way to survive the leaving
is to love whatever is left of yourself,
is to love whatever remains.

This is me moving on. This is me accepting the ache of missing you. This is me waking up every single day and tackling the street corners we walked upon, the corner coffee shops we ate at, the sheets we wrapped ourselves in at night. This is me waking up every single day, aware of what is missing, but accepting of the fact that this is my life now, that this is the way things are going to be. This is me understanding that it is okay to have my heartbeat speak your name. This is me understanding that it is okay to miss someone who was once such a staple in my life. But this is also me understanding that life does go on. That one day I will hear the songs and smile, I will sleep in the sheets and they will no longer smell like you; one day I will fall in love again, one day I will look back on this and my hands will not shake with the heaviness of it all.

This is me moving on. This is me accepting the fact that we will no longer make memories together. This is me coming to terms with the reality of a future without you. This is me understanding that you will do everything we had ever spoken about—you will live a life you are proud of, you will become the person you told me you hoped you could be, you will take the trips, you will experience all of the things you wanted to experience, you will love—deeply and wholly and with every inch of your patchwork heart, but all of that will happen without me by your side.

This is me moving on. This is me accepting that you will, as well. This is me coming to terms with the fact that someone else is going to fall in love with your light, that someone else is going to be your biggest fan. This is me hoping that you will find the love you deserve. This me me hoping that you will find someone who inspires you and moves you and appreciates every stunning thing you are. This is me hoping that you find someone who stirs the deepest parts of your being, someone who is both your safe place and your biggest adventure. This is me hoping that you are happy, truly happy, one day.

This is me moving on. This is me accepting that sometimes beautiful things end. This is me understanding that there is nothing I can say or do to fix that. This is me coming to terms with the fact that sometimes leaving is an act of love, too. That sometimes you have to walk away from something soft and hauntingly real, that sometimes hearts don't align. But this is me accepting that endings don't have to be messy. This is me understanding how incredible it really is—that for a moment in time, in a world of billions, two strangers were in the right place, at the right time, and something transpired between them. This is my heart swelling with the thought—that at one point in time, we were the lucky ones. At one point in time, we beat the odds.

How do you find the right one
in a world of 7 billion people?

First—you become the right one.
The rest will follow.

Listen—whatever it is that makes you wake up, whatever it is that makes you feel a moment of peace or a glimmer of hope, just keep it close. Please, live for it. Make sure that you focus on it. Make sure that you make time for it. I don't care what it is. You have to understand that happiness does not have to be this big all-consuming thing. Sometimes happiness is your morning cup of coffee. Sometimes it is the smell in the street after it rains, or your favorite song played on repeat for three hours straight. Sometimes happiness is your friend's laughter or the way the sky looks through the trees in your favorite park. If it keeps you going, if it ignited something within you, it doesn't matter how small or grand it is. Just hold on to it. Let it save you.

Some of the kindest souls I know have lived in a world that was not so kind to them. Some of the best human beings I know have been through so much at the hands of others, and they still love deeply, they still care. Sometimes, it's the people who have been hurt the most who refuse to be hardened in this world, because they would never want to make another person feel the same way they have felt. If that isn't something to be in awe of, I don't know what is.

What a shame it truly is—
that some of us have lived
our entire lives
under the impression
that the love
we have been searching for
was to be found,
first and foremost,
in anyone but ourselves.

When it comes down to it, I think if any of us are going to make it, we simply just have to believe. We have to believe in the power of the small things—in the comfort of a cup of coffee, in the calming, melted hues of a sunrise, in hearing our mother's voice on the other end of the phone after a long day. We have to believe that we can overcome whatever weight life ropes to our spines, whatever circumstances our choices or our shortcomings throw our way. We have to believe in love; we have to believe that we are worthy of it, that we are deserving of being chosen despite the insecurity or the flaws or the mistakes. We have to believe in our ability to take care of the people we care about; we have to believe that we are enough for them. We have to believe that we have permission to be whomever the hell we want to be, that we have the capacity to be truly, and deeply, happy. We have to believe that we aren't alone, that people see us for who we are and what we have the potential to be. If we're going to make it, we have to believe that we are growing. We have to believe that we are meant to be here.

I hope you know that you are deserving of everything you want in life. You deserve to fall in love with someone who cares for you in the softest way, someone who drives you and believes in you and is always in your corner—not just when it is easy, but when it is hard, too. You deserve to be that person for yourself as well. You deserve to be surrounded by people who grow your mind, people who make you better because they push you to be better. You deserve the kind of confidence that makes you believe that anything is possible, the kind that empowers your voice and your ideas and your capacity to seek out the things that you desire. You deserve moments of pure and intense happiness, the kind that make you feel your heart beating against your chest, the kind that dizzy you and make you realize that everything will be okay. Because it will be. *It will be.* You deserve to be chosen. You deserve to be loved the way you love others. At the end of the day, you deserve to be inspired by your life. I hope you never forget that.

I am no longer afraid of the mess this healing will create.
I am here to unravel.
I am here to unpack these bones.

You are not broken,
you are becoming.

My god, I hope you find love. And I don't just mean that in regards to someone you wrap your tired bones around at night. I mean that I hope you find love in every aspect of your life. I hope you find it tucked into early morning sunrises and the smell of your favorite places. I hope you find it strung between the laughter you share with friends I hope it bounces off of you when you hug the people you care for I hope it swells within your rib cage whenever you hear your favorite song or discover something that moves you. I hope you fall in love with growth, and change, and the messiness, and the beauty of fucking up, and making mistakes, and becoming exactly who you want to be. I hope you find love in places that were once devoid of it, in places within yourself that you could have been softer to, kinder to, in the past. Because if there is one thing I have learned, it is that love is so much more than a boy or a girl who holds your heart. Love is everything around you. It is everything.

It is quite simple. When it comes to anything in life—relationships, friendships, the work you do, the art you make—when it comes to *anything*, if it does not create an avalanche within your chest, if it does not move you and inspire you, if it does not come from the deepest part of who you are, it is not for you. *It is not for you.*

In all honesty, I don't think the world changes—I think you change.

And I don't think the messiness or the ache of living ever goes away; I don't think it ever disappears. I think you just get stronger. I think you just get better at not letting the dark stifle the light. I think you just get better at not letting the chaos control you.

The truth is—sometimes love changes. The truth is, sometimes life gets hard and "I'll stay" turns into "I have to take care of myself right now." Sometimes, those who loved us beautifully cannot continue to do so. And that is okay. You have to understand that there are certain things in life you truly have to let go of. There are certain things in life you cannot control— and the heart of another person is one of them. Either someone chooses you or they do not. Either someone decides to fight or they do not. At the end of the day, you have to respect that. But you do not have to let it consume you. See, you may not be able to control the person you loved, but you can control yourself. You can control the way you unapologetically dedicate yourself to loving who you are and what you have to offer. You can control the way you move forward, the way you choose to believe that you are worthy of the love you have continuously put out into the world. You can control the way you choose to believe that all the love your heart has given was enough and will be enough for the right people. You can control how you grow from the loss. You can control how you survive it. So survive it. You are strong enough to do so.

I am slowly learning what it means to be human.

I am slowly learning how to forgive the past. How to accept that sometimes beautiful things end, that sometimes the timing isn't right, that sometimes the messiness of life gets in the way. I am slowly learning that endings aren't something to be upset about, but rather, I am slowly learning how to appreciate how damn lucky I was to experience something real and hopeful and light in a world that sometimes fails to be soft.

I am slowly learning how to be alone. I am slowly learning how to wake up in the middle of the bed. How to make just one cup of coffee in the mornings. How to hold my own heart, how to take up my own space. I am slowly learning how to stop filling voids with other human beings, and instead, I am slowly learning how to confront the void itself. How to heal it.

I am slowly learning what it means to be human. What it means to make mistakes and learn from them. What it means to be both happy and sad at the same time. I am slowly learning how to do the damn work. How to stop running from what is heavy and uncomfortable in my life. How to take the easy route less and less. How to grow myself, how to be a better person.

But most of all, *I am slowly learning* how to just be in this moment. How to exist. How to understand that I cannot control life, that I can only experience it in both its light and its dark stages. I am slowly learning how to laugh and cry and feel through it all, how to welcome the confusion and the joy that come with loving and living and breaking. I am slowly learning how to accept where I am.

I am slowly learning how to simply believe in the person I am becoming.

The love you find within yourself
will be yours forever.

When you're wondering if loving someone was worth it, ask yourself this. If you could go back in time, if you could do it all over again, would you? Would you choose that person, would you choose that hope, knowing that you would also be choosing that hurt? Knowing that at one point in time, you were going to have to survive the loss of them, the ache of missing? Would you still risk for them? Would you still love them? Would you still stay up until 4 AM with them on the night you met, letting yourself fall? Would you still get on the plane? Would you still forgive and trust; would you still make the memories, would you still give them a home in your heart? See, if the answer is no, then maybe what you had was not love; maybe it was a lesson. Maybe you can find closure in that. But if your answer is yes, then ah—do not doubt if it was worth it. Do not make it any less beautiful in your mind, do not turn it into something you choose to forget. No, if you would do it all again, if you would still choose just a few more hours, just a few more days, just a few more years, despite the inevitable loss, then you had something most people never find in this lifetime. You had something worth the fight.

So this is your life, and you are going to be both moved and confused by it. You are going to experience things that will inspire you and things that you will never quite come to terms with. You are going to love people that you will sometimes lose, but you will also find those who stay. Appreciate those people; let them know that you care. You are going to laugh until you cry; you're going to ache in ways you never thought possible; you are going to be exhausted by the chaos of it all and ignited by the beauty. You are going to be hurt, and you are going to hurt. Sometimes you will be the bad person. Sometimes you will be the one who makes the mistake. Sometimes you will have to give yourself your own closure. Sometimes you will have to let go. Sometimes you will have to find comfort in being alone, in being lost. Yes, this is your life, and though it can be unpredictable and messy, though it can break you down—you are going to survive it. You will always survive it.

Don't break your own heart
trying to fill someone else's.

And above all else—
I hope whatever you love, loves you back.

Please, just tell people how you feel, and do not worry about being too much. Be too much. Care too much. Hope too much. Give too much. Give everything you have. If you feel like you have loved someone to the best of your ability—love them more. Love them more than you could ever imagine, because if there is anything I have learned, it is that we need each other. We need each other.

I think it's brave. I think it's brave that you get up in the morning when your heart aches and life is messy and you do not feel like being soft for the world. I think it is brave that you continue to love and express and open your soul, despite the way you were treated in the past. I think it is brave that you keep going, that you keep believing in something more, something bigger, even when you may not know what you are hoping for. I think it is brave that you fight, I think it is brave that you choose, every single day, to move forward—because that is what makes you strong. That is what makes you strong.

When the weight of living
hangs heavy on your spine,
you must remind yourself:

"Other people feel this, too.
Other people feel this, too."

You have to envision it, no matter how hard life fights you. You have to see yourself out of the messiness, out of the dark. You have to envision it—you in Paris, or Rome, or wherever the hell your heart wants to go, with your best friend, feeling like the whole world is opening up for you. You have to envision it—the small apartment in your favorite city that you share with someone who is your biggest fan, the both of you sitting on the couch sipping coffee and reminiscing about all of the small and nameless things you got to share together. You have to envision it—the mornings you wake up and there is no heaviness in your chest, no lump in your throat. You have to envision it—the survival. The hope. The version of yourself you can't, and won't, give up on. You have to envision it; you have to hold on to whatever it is that fills you with courage, because the world needs you here. It needs you.

Love will not save you. But it will hold your hand while you save yourself. And in a world that sometimes seems devoid of goodness, in a world that sometimes feels too heavy to bear, I think that is all we are really searching for. Someone by our side. Someone who grounds us. Someone who will quietly hug us for twenty minutes straight while we figure it all out. I think that is all anyone really needs. Someone who sees them. Someone who stays.

Make your life art.
Make it something
you are proud of.

Learn how to be with yourself fully and without reservation or discomfort. Learn how to love yourself the way you love others—embrace all of your flaws, all of your darkness; cheer on your accomplishments, don't downplay your wins. Turn every mistake you make into something forgivable. Hold yourself and heal yourself; trust in the fact that you have the capacity to rescue whatever part of you needs saving. Please, just show yourself some grace, just show up. Because life gets hard and people leave, but you will always have yourself. You will always be your own home.

There is more to life than the person who walked away from you. There is more to life than chasing after someone who does not want to be in yours.

Trust me when I say—there is more to life.

There is laughing until your stomach aches more than your healing.

There is going out with friends and kissing their faces and talking to them about atoms and the universe and the fact that you are so damn lucky to be living at the same time as them, that you are so damn thankful you got to experience life with them by your side. They'll scoop you into their arms and they will hug you so tight that it will feel as if all of your broken pieces have finally come together again.

There are warm summer evenings where the skies are dusted in rose and peach, the kind of evenings that feel like salt water for your soul, the kind of evenings that cleanse you and hold you and make you feel so small and so big at the same time.

There are corner coffee shops with mugs in every shade of feeling where you will read the paper and pretend that you're in Paris or Spain and sip too strong coffee as you learn to be alone.

There are crystallizing moments in the middle of crowds where you will connect with the fact that your hands don't feel as heavy anymore, that your heart is floating above water for the first time in months, that you feel happy and light and full of hope.

But most of all—there is you, in all of your glory and heart, learning how to love yourself day by day. There is you, in all of your depth, living and feeling and existing despite the hurt, despite the loss. There is you being your own person, being your own strength. There is you being there for yourself, for the first time in a long time. There is you finding your own happiness.

Now *that* is something worth chasing. *That* is something to care about.

Remember the ones who loved you back;
remember the ones who stayed.

You have to believe that there are still good people left in this world. Because there are. There are people who will show up for you and care for you. There are people who mean it when they say that they will stay. There are people who would never think of hurting you, who would never think of leaving you behind. There are still people you can trust; there are still people who are tender and kind and honest. And I know that you have been hurt before, and I know that every gentle part of you wants to give up on believing, but you must. You must. Because they exist, and you will find them. Don't ever stop trusting in that; don't ever stop searching.

Maybe you don't end up with the person your heart chooses. Maybe that's not how life works. Maybe you don't get what you want. Maybe you end up finding what you need, and maybe the universe knows what you need more than you do.

Maybe love changes. Maybe it goes from "I'll wait up and call you after work" to "I'm going to sleep, I'm tired." Maybe it goes from "You have nothing to worry about" to "I really wish you didn't overthink so much." Maybe it goes from "I choose you" to "I have to choose myself right now."

Maybe love isn't one of those things that grows with certain people. Maybe you become too big for it. Maybe it becomes too uncomfortable, too small for who you change into. Maybe it's like that sweater you always loved growing up or your childhood bed. You learn to appreciate it for what it was, but you come to terms with the fact that you have outgrown it. You learn to let it go.

And maybe letting go of love isn't some loud celebration at the end of a dark tunnel. Maybe letting go is the moment you decide that you can no longer keep the past alive inside of you. Maybe it is quiet, maybe there is no checklist or way of telling if it has actually happened. Maybe it is simply just you learning how to release your grip, how to let things be, how to lay down your arms. Maybe that is how it's done—in the silence of it all, in the calmness of everyday life.

I am starting to learn that maybe walking away is the best thing you can do for yourself and for the person you love. Maybe walking away is you making peace with the fact that sometimes things and people and happiness change. Maybe it is the bravest thing you can do. Maybe when you walk away, you're not making the biggest mistake of your life. Maybe when you walk away, your life is just beginning.

Just be gentle. Be gentle because we all have worlds inside of ourselves that no one else sees. And some of us, some of our worlds are heavy right now. Some of our worlds are filled with darkened hope, some of our worlds are filled with hurt—they lack the magic they once did. So just be gentle, because you never know which world someone holds inside of themselves. You never know someone's story.

What a shame it is—
that we are so quick
to find a soul mate
before we take the time
to find, and truly understand,
our own souls.

See, growth isn't this comfortable, miraculous thing. It can get ugly, it can get confusing. It's gritty, it's hard. It's difficult to confront yourself sometimes; it's difficult to be the person who does things differently, who doesn't settle. But it's the greatest gift you will ever give yourself. It will push you towards figuring out what your own personal version of happiness looks like; and when you grow on your own terms, when you figure out what actually matters to you, and when you carve out your own path, you live on your own terms. You love on your own terms. You become the person you have always wanted to be, rather than the person you were always told to be, and that is beautiful. Because when it comes down to it—life is about making yourself proud on your own terms. It's about finding a happiness that works for you.

You are not what you are going through.
You are not what you are going through.
You are not what you are going through.

Let me tell you about people who love deeply.

They are wells of feeling. Storms of hope and heart that never know when to stop the downpour. People who love deeply are both soft and strong; they are whirlwinds of rarity that will only ever know how to empty themselves out for the people they love. People who love deeply do not know how to turn their hearts off, do not know how to stop giving, and though this is the most beautiful aspect of who they are, it is also the most fatal, for people who love deeply also hurt deeply.

See, people who love deeply always lock the hurricane that is their soul into the wrong rib cages. They spill out into the bones of people who were only ever hoping to be a temporary home for their warmth; they deplete all of their emotion just trying to fill the hollowness in those who do not appreciate it.

When it comes to people who love deeply, the ones they choose can't quite understand just how someone could pour themselves out for another person and ask for nothing in return. However, they do not set them free. They continue to take. They continue to accept a love they know they could never possibly mirror. They allow for the warmth of this human being to make them feel new again, and when they are done with the keeping of a rare and beautiful thing, only then do they discard it. Only then do they tell it that it is no longer needed.

But people who love deeply have a hard time being set free. Not because they are weak, not because it is in their nature to beg for the admiration of others, no. People who love deeply have a hard time leaving because they can never quite convince themselves that they need to walk away from someone they know they can help. They will never stop trying to love someone into their potential, will never stop falling for the echo of "what if" in another human being.

And this is where people who love deeply hurt the most. In the small ache that forms in their chest, the unfinished business that creates caverns of confusion in their minds. They wonder if they were good enough, and the thought of someone leaving when they still had so much left to give haunts them for the rest of their lives. They never forget. People who love deeply never forget—they are tattooed with the goodbyes of everyone they never got the chance to shine for. Even if the love was wrong, to someone who loves deeply, no amount of loving is a waste, no amount of taking is too much. They live to give.

That is where you come in. Let me tell you about people who love deeply—they are human beings that don't quite make sense to most. They are the few genuine souls who give and do not need to be filled in return. They are resources of boundless feeling, but that does not mean you get to take advantage of that. No, if you do not respect that, if you do not know when to stop taking and when to start loving them despite their inability to ask for that love, do not touch them. Do not taste them. Do not drink from the well of their hope. Do not be selfish with their heart. Do not ruin them like the others.

Fall in love with someone who is
both your safe place
and your biggest adventure.

When the world is quiet and you're truly alone and with your mind, what do you think about? What do you hope for? Follow that.

Here's what they don't tell you—you're never really going to figure it out. You're never going to figure out the world, or why the things that happened to you happened, or how to ensure that your future is faultless. You're never going to figure out how to perfect your existence, because it was never meant to be perfected. Instead, you will figure out how to move forward, day by day. You will figure out what kind of breakfast you like in the morning and what kind of people you want by your side. You will figure out the places that make your soul feel at home, and sometimes those places will be human beings. You will figure out what ignites your passion, the things that you could see yourself doing every single day for ten, or twenty, or thirty years. You'll figure out how to say no and how to stand up for yourself. You'll figure out how to forgive and let go. You'll figure out exactly how you like to take your coffee. You'll figure out how to walk away, how to heal. You'll figure out how to live with yourself, how to be your own companion. You'll figure out how to be kind to even the most broken parts of yourself. See, you'll figure out how to embrace life. How to truly accept it as it comes. And it won't always be easy or clean-cut; it won't always make sense, and you won't always have control. But it will be yours. It will be yours.

What is the point in being alive if you are not going to try for something? If you are not going to at least attempt to make your time here remarkable? Stop holding yourself back. Tell the person that makes your stomach ache with hope that every part of your heart is tender for them, even if you think you have no chance. Don't just fantasize about your dream job— actively pursue it, and if that door is not open, knock it down. Buy the plane ticket, jump the fence, kiss the stranger. Make sure that you don't allow your fear to hold you back. Instead, look your fear in the face and invite it to dinner, become its best friend. Live along-side it, let it make you feel alive. Please, just choose impossibility. Choose risk. Choose making mistakes and making memories and making it up as you go. Just choose to embrace whatever time you do have here, because life is finite, and fragile, and it vanishes too quickly. Make it worth it. Make it count.

I wish I could explain what healing feels like. I wish I could tell you that it feels like coming home, that it feels like every soft and tender thing you have ever held within your hands. I wish I could tell you that healing is the simplest art form, that it is the act of doing this or that, that it is an equation you could master if you just focused on forgiveness, if you just flayed the hurt from your bone. But healing will never be artistic, it will never be delicate, because healing is the messiest thing you will ever know. Healing feels like digging the dirt out of your soul, like making room for yourself within your own body. Healing feels like the shining of a flickering light into the caverns life has managed to create within you; it feels like picking out the broken pieces one by one. Healing will never be linear, it will never make sense. One day you will have the answers clenched between your palms, and the next you will melt into the kitchen floor, you will ask for the world to be quieter for a while. Healing will start in the morning, and it will end at night, and no day will ever be the same. There will never be a formula. You will simply begin the process again when the sun rises. You will embark on daily journeys. You will take your steps forward. You will take your steps back. But you will always be moving, and that is what you need to celebrate.

I need you to know that it gets better.

I need you to know that the way you flay your heart open for the world is brave, that the way in which you refuse to be anything but soft, even when you feel like you may just break under the weight of feeling, is why you are needed here. I need you to know that beautiful things are vanishing each day, and I am proud of you for fighting to ensure that your soul is not one of them. You need to keep fighting.

I need you to know that you will find the places that leave every tender part of you feeling calm and at peace with who you are. You will find the places that inspire everything inside of you to surge and ache with the hope and the beauty of being alive. These places, they are not where you were born, but they will be where you are reborn. You will know when you have found them. My god, will you know.

I need you to know that there are others like you in this world; others who are messy-hearted, others who feel things intensely and without hesitation, others who cannot contain all that they hold within the worlds of their mind because they have only ever known how to pour, how to shatter, how to give and give and give. I need you to know that you will find these people, and they will become your family—you will take care of each other. You will grow together in the moments between breaths, in the stunning silence that blankets your souls when you connect with the fact that in a world of billions, in the middle of all this noise, you found each other.

But most of all, I need you to know that we are all here, together, dealing with what is dark and light within us. I need you to know that you aren't alone. I need you to know that you are going to survive this. I need you to know that one day, you're going to be sitting in a place you love, surrounded by people who inspire you, and you're going to think back to the storms and the hurricanes that rattled through your bones, and you are going to smile. The clarity will wash over you.

You will be free. You will be free.

You're going to realize it one day—that happiness was never about your job or your degree or being in a relationship. Happiness was never about following in the footsteps of all of those who came before you; it was never about being like the others. One day, you're going to see it—that happiness was always about the discovery, the hope, the listening to your heart and following it wherever it chose to go. Happiness was always about being kinder to yourself; it was always about embracing the person you were becoming. One day, you will understand that happiness was always about learning how to live with yourself, that your happiness was never in the hands of others. It was always about you. It was always about you.

Love is quite possibly the only thing that can both build and break a human being, and that makes moving on difficult. Remind yourself that it is often the highlights that leave you longing for the past, the good memories, the beautiful moments, the building blocks —but there were also the downfalls, the breaks, the things that caused the relationship to end in the first place. There are so many breathtaking people in the world, people who have the potential to create with you something that is foundational, something that drives and inspires you to be a better person. Open yourself up to them; open yourself up to the kind of love you deserve.

Pay more attention to what stirs your heart. Pay attention to the music that makes you want to cry, or dance, or jump right out of your skin. Pay attention to what makes you happy—truly happy, the kind of happy that drips from your bones, the kind of happy that gives you hope and makes you believe that you have a reason to be here. Pay attention to the things that make you laugh, the things that make you smile. Really focus on figuring out what compels you, really focus on discovering the aspects of the world that interest you and challenge you and make you want to learn and grow. You have to pay attention. To the things that make you believe in being alive, to the people that support you and build you up and make you feel like you're understood in a world that can sometimes feel like a haunted and hurtful place. You have to pay attention to the life you want to create for yourself, because you are in charge of your own happiness, you are in charge of who you become. So, if something makes your heart feel like it is finally home—pay attention to it. Whether it is a job, or a hobby, or a person, or a place—just follow it. Just make your life your own.

Some days I feel like the person
I have always wanted to be,
and other days
I can feel my heart breaking
for all of the past versions of myself
I let down
when I chose not to protect
all that they were
when I chose to tell them
that they were not good enough.

At the end of the day, I just want to be proud of the person I have become. I want to be proud of the love I gave—of the way in which I risked my heart despite being hurt. I want to be proud of the effort I showed those I cared about; I want to know with a ruthless certainty that I showed up as much as I could, that I made people feel seen, that I made those around me feel less alone in this chaotic world. I want to be proud of my life—of the way I healed, of the way I made mistakes and learned from them, of the way I felt everything even when it wasn't convenient or comfortable. I want to be proud of the way I grew, of the way I let go, of the way I pushed myself to be a better person. At the end of the day, I just want to be able to say without hesitation that I lived my life, that I did not just take a back seat to my pain, or to my flaws, or to whatever hardships came my way. I want to be able to say that I am proud of the way I survived. I want to be able to say that I did not take one day for granted.

One day you're going to wake up and your heart won't be beating out of your chest for all of the wrong reasons. One day you're going to cook breakfast to your favourite song and you're not going to feel like the walls are closing in on you. One day you're going to look in the mirror and you're not going to recognize the person looking back at you, because you changed. You changed, and that is the single greatest reality of moving forward; that is the incredible outcome of surviving the hardest parts of your journey.

And yes, sometimes life is going to kick your teeth in. Sometimes it is going to confuse you, sometimes nothing will make sense and everything will be messy. But you're going to learn. You're going to fight tooth and nail, and you're going to grow. Slowly but surely, you're going to grow.

You're going to find your people. You're going to stay up until 5 AM on a random Tuesday and talk about your past with someone who enlivens you. You may even fall in love. You're going to go to concerts that ring truth through your bones and make you feel like your cells are vibrating. You're going to stop and stare at the ocean and you're going to feel so small, yet so fucking big, and you're going to finally, *finally*, feel like things are falling into place. You're going to be moved by your life. You're going to feel everything all at once—you're going to feel complete.

Trust me when I say that one day it's going to hit you—that you woke up happy, that you're smiling for no reason, that your hands aren't shaking anymore. One day, you're going to remember what it was like to be you a year ago, or three years ago, or even a week ago, and you're going to be so glad that you fought. You're going to be so glad that you kept going.

Maybe you don't
always get what you want.
Maybe sometimes
you get something
far greater
than anything
you could have ever hoped for.

You give all your love to others,
but sometimes you forget
that you deserve it, too.

You are going to find them—the person who under-stands just what it means to be in love with the soft-ness you hold between your palms. You are going to find them—the person who comprehends the brevity of a soul that aches with hope and overflows with the feeling to a point of destruction sometimes. You are going to find them, and they will understand when you are anxious, or overwhelmed, or when you just need to fold into the corners of your heart for a few hours. They will understand that the past broke you, and built you, and left you to navigate the mess of what it means to be a human that has loved and lost and trusted with every inch of their being. They will understand. On your good days and on your bad days. On the days when you are a shining example of everything you want to be and on the days when you shrink into your healing. I promise you—they will come along, and you will know because your bones will ache with knowing. You will know because your heart will recognize itself in the heart of someone else. You will know, because for once, you won't be afraid. Everything will be calm, and something deep within you will soften, something deep within you will say, "it is time."

I hope you learn how to love yourself the way you love others—unconditionally and without hesitation; deeply, and from the softest parts of who you are. Because isn't it a shame that we are so quick to forgive the humanness in someone else's soul, but we often forget to forgive ourselves? Isn't it a shame that we fight for others, we believe in them with such intensity, and such hope, but we often forget to fight for ourselves?

I am proud of you. I am proud of you for trying, even when it hurts. It takes a lot to be the kind of person who challenges themselves to change; it takes a lot to be the kind of person who confronts all that is lost and haunted within them. I wish I could tell you when you will know, when your head will finally feel like it is floating above water, but healing is something you will never be able to time; it is something you will never be able to measure. Things will get lighter as you break up the earth within yourself. Things will get lighter as you excavate the past from your mind, when you learn how to forgive it and befriend it. So keep taking the steps. Keep asking the questions. Keep facing the things you need to face. You are getting closer every single day, even when it does not feel that way.

Be thankful for all that did not work out in your life. When you felt like you lost a human soul, when you gripped at its being, when you wished for it to stay— you gained space; and within that space you understood that the person you so deeply longed for did not meet your heart on its own level, did not try the way you tried, did not ache the way you ached. When you felt like you missed an opportunity, a pathway, a finish line on your journey—clarity bloomed within you, and you learned how to give yourself permission to change, you learned how to give yourself permission to make mistakes and overcome them, permission to take a different path, to dream a different dream. See, at the end of the day, all that you have lost is all that you have gained. The universe does not leave you empty; it always balances the scales within you. For all that it takes, it gives. For all that it destroys, it creates. Reassess all that you think is damaged and defeated within you. Every breakdown was just a step forward into your becoming.

I am learning
how to be soft
for all of the hands
that want to hold me
(including my own).

I know that it is hard to forgive when your chest feels like the broken ruins of a city that was once intact. I know that it is hard to forgive when you feel the fragments of every memory crashing around in your lungs, churning within you whenever you try to breathe in clean air. I know that it is hard to walk forward each day with the heaviness that exists inside of you right now, but you must understand this. Anger is not going to sweep the ashes from your bones. Resentment is not going to mend the ache, not going to shine a light into all that is cracked within you. Holding on to all of this destruction, clenching it within your palms, is never going to turn it to dust, is never going to absolve you of its presence. Only you will do that for yourself. Only you will resurrect your heart. Because forgiveness is never about those who wronged you or broke you; it is never about those who could not see your value, who could not protect you. Forgiveness has always been about learning how to give yourself the closure you seek in others. Forgiveness has always been about learning how to accept the things you cannot change. Forgiveness has always been about learning how to befriend your past rather than making it an enemy. Forgiveness has always been about you. It has always been about you.

A soul mate does not complete you—they inspire you to complete yourself. A soul mate is the person who supports your direction, who motivates and encourages you to stretch, to change, to reinvent yourself until you are happy. A soul mate is someone who loves you with so much conviction, and so much heart, that it is nearly impossible to doubt just how capable you are of becoming exactly who you have always wanted to be.

What a shame it is
to mistake gentleness for weakness.
To be soft is to be strong.
To be soft is to be strong.

Live a life that is driven—
not by fear, but by love.

If you're the person who is always there for others, know that your heart is rare. Know that you give people hope. Know that you make people feel wanted, that you make people feel seen; know that you make people feel like they have purpose. However, also remind yourself that you are not invincible. Your heart needs rest. You need rest. Remind yourself that you do not need to carry the weight of the world on your shoulders, that you may not be able to save everyone, that you may not be able to heal every hurt. Remind yourself that you deserve to take all of the energy you put out into the world and invest it back into yourself from time to time. That you are worthy of the love you keep giving to everyone else. Remind yourself that you don't always have to be strong, that you don't always have to be the fixer. You can be human; you can ask for help. You can take a step back to nourish the softness inside of you.

You are here to make the best of it. To discover things that move you deeply. To feel things you have never felt before. You are here to meet people who ignite your mind, people who connect with your very soul. You are here to live a life you're proud of, to find all that exists in this world that was made for you. And if there ever comes a time where you do not feel like there is art bursting from every part of who you are, I hope you have the courage to start over. I hope you have the strength to become the person you truly want to be.

But here's the thing—you can't keep choosing someone who doesn't choose you. You can't. Because your person is going to be your person for the rest of your life. Not just when you're young and things are perfect, but when things get messy and you make mistakes and the world is less shiny. You have to make sure that you have someone by your side that wants to be there. Someone who wants to support you, and encourage you. Someone who gives you just as much effort as you give them. Someone who wants to hear your laugh, and make breakfast with you, and listen to all of your dumb jokes for twenty or thirty or fifty years. Because there are difficult things in life, really hard and haunted things that make it heavy and hurtful at times. But love should not be one of those things. Love should hold your hand and help you brave those storms. Love should be your safe place. So please, just don't give the best parts of yourself to someone who doesn't see the value in what they are receiving. Don't settle for anyone who doesn't look at you and know, without hesitation, that they want to stay.

Sometimes, the greatest act of self-love is simply allowing yourself to be loved by others. Sometimes, the greatest act of self-love is simply allowing yourself to be seen in all that you are.

If you feel like you cannot move on from whatever you are going through at the moment, remember this: Six months ago, or twelve months ago, or two years ago, you thought the same. You were in a position that threatened all that was hopeful within you; you did not think you would survive. But six months ago, or twelve months ago, or two years ago—you did. You did. You woke up in the morning. You pushed through the mess; you dug yourself out of the hurt. You held on to whatever light you found within your days; you pressed it into yourself whenever you could, reminding yourself that goodness still existed, that the softness was still there. Six months ago, or twelve months ago, or two years ago, you fought your way out of the dark. You have the strength to save yourself. You always have. Please don't ever forget that.

Remember this, repeat it every single day:

You cannot love someone into loving you
if they do not.

Be the reason why
someone believes in the goodness and in the heart
of other human beings.

Please, whatever you do—just feel what you are feeling right now. Do not reach into yourself and pull out what life has planted within you. Instead, reach into yourself and cradle it. Give it a home within you. Let it stay for as long as it needs. Do not rush it out the door. Just be with it. Whatever it is—whether it is a name, or a memory, or an ache that you cannot seem to part with. Do not harden yourself to what has affected you so deeply in life. This is the important part. Be thankful for it. Be thankful for the songs you hear that make your soul bubble over with nostalgia. Be thankful for the morning light and how it hits that one spot on your bed that holds the ghosted memory of someone who was once your favorite thing. Be thankful for your heart and how at one point you could feel it beating against your rib cage for ten days straight because your bones were blushing at the thought of someone's hand within yours. Let these moments seek refuge in your soul. Let them wash over you. Let them remind you that at one point, you embraced what it meant to love without abandon. Let them remind you that at one point, you tried for something.

I wish I could tell you that you have to do it a certain way. That you have to read a certain book or take a certain trip. That you will be rewarded with a moment of beauty that changes your life, that unlocks the happiness inside of you, if you just do this or that. I wish I could tell you that you will heal in four months, or two weeks, or by next Monday if you really try. But I can't. I can't. For if there is anything I have learned about moving forward, about letting go, about becoming the person you want to become—it is that it happens in the quietest moments. Growth creeps into you, it burrows and it stretches, it cracks you open from the inside, and one day you wake up and you really connect with the fact that you are happy to have opened your eyes. One day you wake up and all you feel is intense love; you almost don't know how to deal with all of the softness blooming from your fingertips. Hope pours out of you onto sidewalks, and into the arms of your lover, and into the words you write and the art you make and the depth of your laughter. You feel so damn lucky to be alive, and you don't really know how it happened or when it did. You don't really know where the shift occurred or what was responsible for it. But I don't think you ever will—because happiness was never something you were going to find. Instead, it was something you were going to become.

The timing is not wrong.
The love is wrong.

I asked her what happiness felt like,
to which she replied,

"It feels like everything inside of you
has become light again,
like for the first time in years,
your heart has finally learned
how to float above water."

If there is one thing I know, it is that life goes on. People change, and love transforms, and our hearts break and grow within us. The things we once wanted fade into new hope, we lose those we thought we would never lose, and we walk away from those we thought we would never walk away from. If there is one thing I know, it is that even through all of its confusion, even through the messiness of our existence, life continues. We push on.

BIANCA SPARACINO is a writer from Toronto.
She wrote this for you.

instagram.com/rainbowsalt
facebook.com/rainbowsalt
thoughtcatalog.com/bianca-sparacino

```
THOUGHT
CATALOG
Books
```

Thought Catalog Books is a publishing house owned by The Thought & Expression Company, an independent media group based in Brooklyn, NY. Founded in 2010, we are committed to facilitating thought and expression. We exist to help people become better communicators and listeners in order to engender a more exciting, attentive, and imaginative world. We are powered by Collective World, a community of creatives and writers from all over the globe.

Visit us on the web at *thoughtcatalog.com* or explore more of our books at *shopcatalog.com*. If you'd like to join our community, apply at *www.collective.world*.

Printed in Great Britain
by Amazon